sh

Sounds & Letters 14

T0025478

KNOWLEDGE
BOOKS

shop	shoe
shed	sheep
ship	shack
shark	

sh

shop

shoe

4

shed

sheep

ship

shack

shark

shop	shoe
shed	sheep
ship	shack
shark	

Knowledge Books and Software
PO Box 50 Sandgate, Queensland 4017 Australia
p. +617-55680288 f. +617-55680277 email: sales@kbs.com.au

First Published 2022
ISBN 9781922516862
Text and editing: Carole Crimeen
Design and layout: Suzanne Fletcher
Publisher: Robert Watts

Series Information: **Sounds and Letters**

Credits
Photographs: Cover © Jeanette Virginia Goh; p. 1 © Dzha33, Grigorev Mikhail, heliopix, Red
Moccasin; p. 3 © FamVeld; p. 5 © erbitsky Denis; p. 7 © pearcec; p. 9 © Baronb; p. 11 © Denis
Belitsky; p. 13 © Jason Brubacher; p. 15 © Digital Storm/Shutterstock.

Phonic support books are a wonderful resource for emergent readers as they encourage independent reading and help students make the link between letters and the sounds they represent.

Have students identify the images on the title page to listen for the sound that they will hear through the book.

Encourage students to point to each word as they read through the book.

ISBN: 9781922516862

9 781922 516862 >

KNOWLEDGE BOOKS

Sounds &
Letters